OLD CUPAR

by

Paula Martin & Steven Penrice

Cupar floods, 8 July 1916, when 3.6 inches of rain fell in 36 hours. This was the first major local flood to be photographed. Here the Lady Burn has overflowed onto Burnside. The heart of the old town of Cupar stands on a hill, safe from floods, but as the town expanded from the late eighteenth century onwards, industrial buildings and poorer housing came to be built in areas more liable to flooding from both the Lady Burn and the Eden.

ISBN 1 84033 036 8

Acknowledgements

The authors would like to thank Shauna Penrice, Colin Martin, Cupar Public
Library, St Andrews University Library, and all the many individuals
in and around Cupar who have helped us in various ways.
The publishers would like to thank Ian Lindsay and Eric Eunson
for making additional pictures available for use in the book.

The publishers regret that they cannot supply
copies of any pictures featured in this book.

Bibliography

Fife Herald; *Fife News Almanac*; *Fifeshire Journal*
Gifford, John, *The Buildings of Scotland: Fife*, London, 1988
Innes, G., *Historical Notes and Reminiscences of Cupar*, Cupar, 1884
Martin, Paula, *Cupar, A Short History and Guide*, published privately, Cupar, 1994
Pride, Glen, *The Kingdom of Fife: An Illustrated Architectural Guide*, Edinburgh, 1990
The Statistical Account of Scotland, Vol. X, Fife, Grant I .R. and Withrington D. J.
(eds.), Wakefield, 1978
New Statistical Account of Scotland, Vol IX, Fife - Kinross, Edinburgh & London, 1845
The Third Statistical Account of Scotland, The County of Fife, Alexander Smith (ed.),
Edinburgh and London, 1952
Trades Directories, various, local and national

The Mercat Cross, *c.*1900. The cross is the symbol of a burgh's right to hold markets. Cupar had a weekly market for food, agricultural and consumer goods, a regular cattle market, plus occasional specific markets for sheep and horses, and eight annual fairs. Most markets filled a large part of the Crossgate, though fish was always sold from the steps of the cross. During the eighteenth and nineteenth centuries there were various plans for a covered market area, but with the exception of the Corn Exchange, built in 1861-62 for the buying and selling of grain, these came to nothing. The shaft of the cross is dated 1683, but the unicorn is a modern replica. The cross originally stood nearer the south side of the Crossgate and its former position is marked by a hexagon of cobbles. In 1812 it was removed to the top of Tarvit Hill, according to one story after the Provost of Cupar lost it to Colonel Wemyss of Wemysshall (now Hill of Tarvit) during a drinking and gambling session. In 1897, by public request, it was given back to the town. After being carefully dismantled and transported by Mr Houston of Hillside Foundry, the unicorn and shaft were re-erected on their present site, on a new base, to celebrate the Diamond Jubilee of Queen Victoria.

INTRODUCTION

Cupar was the county town of Fife until local government reorganisation in 1975. It was the home of the sheriff and his court by 1213, and had become a royal burgh by 1328. Lying at the eastern end of the Howe of Fife, the town provided a crossing point over the River Eden, and was the hub of a network of roads, including the 'Great Road', linking the Forth ferries from Edinburgh with the Tay ferries to Dundee. As roads were improved and more people travelled, Cupar became increasingly important as a place to rest, eat and change horses. The building of St Catherine Street enabled larger hotels with ample stabling to be built, the first Tontine Hotel in about 1812 and the Royal, at one time 'the largest Posting Establishment in Fife', in 1854.

The prosperity of Cupar was based on its twin functions as a major market town and a legal centre. In the Middle Ages its merchants traded with northern Europe, exporting surplus agricultural products such as wool and hides, and importing luxury goods like wine and dried fruit. But the town could not compete with maritime burghs such as Crail or Dysart, and was gradually commercially eclipsed by Kirkcaldy and Dunfermline. It had always been overshadowed by St Andrews as a cultural centre. By the mid-nineteenth century, the development of a railway network allowed the exploitation of coal from inland areas of west Fife, and the balance of population shifted dramatically towards the western part of the county. While Cupar remained the county town, sheriff courts were also established in Dunfermline and Kirkcaldy. More and more of the county organisation was gradually moved to Kirkcaldy, and after local government reorganisation in 1975, Fife Regional Council was run from Fife House in Glenrothes; Cupar became the administrative centre of North East Fife District. It is now only about the tenth largest town in Fife.

As the county town, Cupar often had troops billeted in it, either on their way somewhere, or to help keep the peace locally. From the late eighteenth century it was also the home of the Fifeshire Militia and Volunteers, and later of local units of the Territorial Army. During the First World War training camps for the Lowland Mounted Brigade were located in Cupar, and during the Second World War Polish troops were billeted in the town.

Medieval Cupar consisted of two parishes, St Mary's with a church to the north-west of the present town, and St Michael of Tarvit, to the south-east. St Mary's was replaced in 1415 by a new church built within the town of Cupar, and dedicated to St Christopher. The tower of this church survives, topped by a spire which was added by the Rev. William Scott in 1620. In 1618 the two parishes were formally united, and in 1785 the present parish church was built. By 1837 the congregation had expanded to such an extent that a second church was needed, and St Michael's was built at the West Port. The later eighteenth and nineteenth centuries also saw the establishment of a number of non-conformist churches such as the First Relief Church, Boston United Presbyterian and the Baptist Church. These, and other congregations, occupied various premises in the town as their numbers grew or declined.

A plan of Cupar survives from 1642. The main change to the town centre following that date was the demolition of the old tolbooth in about 1815 so that St Catherine Street could be built to provide a more impressive entrance to the town from the east. But while the street plan has survived largely intact, very few of the buildings date from before the middle of the eighteenth century. There was a major rebuilding phase in the 1760s and another in the first years of the nineteenth century. Most of this took place within the existing town boundary, by increasing the height of the buildings fronting the street, and by adding more buildings in the closes and courts behind. During the eighteenth century a few industrial premises moved out beyond the South Bridge and down by Burnside. By the nineteenth century there were also housing developments, such as Riggs Place, Newtown and Castlefield, being built outside the old town.

A few early photographs show Cupar in the 1860s, although the majority date from 1895 onwards. During the 1860s, when photography was in its infancy, there were at least four commercial photographers working in Cupar. Following this rush of early enthusiasm there were only two photographers in the town during the rest of the nineteenth century. One was Robert Heggie (1827-1904), who trained as a lithographer at the *Fife Herald* office. He set up in business on his own at 40 Crossgate, and from c.1869 to 1894 also worked as a photographer from a studio at 6 South Bridge. The other was David Gordon. A shoemaker by trade, in 1864 he set up as a photographer in Kirkcaldy, opening a branch in Leven in 1866. In 1873 he took over Henry Adamson's studio in New Road, Cupar, later working from addresses in Hood Park, Bonnygate and Kirk Wynd, until his death in 1916.

Often photographs can be dated by the buildings shown in them. The Corn Exchange and its spire date from 1862, the Duncan Institute from 1870, the Mercat Cross was restored to the Cross in 1897, and the war memorial was erected in 1922. While the town of Cupar has changed remarkably little, there is still much of interest to be found in old photographs of the town, particularly in the many aspects of its social history that have been recorded.

Cupar folk celebrating the relief of Mafeking, 1900. Mafeking was one of three places in southern Africa where British garrisons had been besieged by the Boers during the Boer War. On May 17, the British general Frederick S. Roberts succeeded in raising the siege after 217 days, a victory which led to widespread public celebration in Britain. The hero of the siege of Mafeking was Robert Baden-Powell (1857-1941), founder of the Boy Scouts. The Boer War (1899-1902) was a conflict between Britain and the Dutch-descended population (Boers) of southern Africa, sparked by disputes over possession of land. The disputes became particularly acrimonious following the discovery of gold in the Boer republic of Transvaal in 1886, which led to an influx of British fortune-hunters.

Proclamation, Cupar, Fife.

The proclamation of the death of one monarch and the accession of the next, probably George V's accession following the death of Edward VII in 1910. This was a ceremony which had been performed in every burgh since its foundation, and only died out between the two world wars with the advent of mass media. The market cross was the symbolic centre of the town's life, both commercial and political, and was also used for other formal proclamations such as the declaration of war.

Market day, Cupar, *c.*1920. This view, looking down on the Mercat Cross and its lamps, shows farmers in the street outside the Corn Exchange. After conducting their business the farmers continued their discussions in the street, or in the Imperial Bar across the road.

St Catherine Street looking west, *c.*1905. On the left is the Tontine Hotel, built *c.*1836 and demolished in 1925 in order to extend the County Buildings. A tontine was an annuity shared by a group of people who had taken out a loan together. Tontines were often bought by people who were setting up a business together, and when one member of the group died their shares were distributed amongst the survivors. This arrangement was frequently used to establish hotels as it prevented interference by heirs who might not understand the business, and might even disapprove of the sale and consumption of alcohol. After the developer of St Catherine Street went bankrupt in 1815 a group of businessmen formed a tontine to get the work finished. In the 1870s the proprietor of the Tontine Hotel, James Hain, advertised 'Superior Hearses with Plumes, with one or four Black Horses, and Mourning Coaches on moderate terms'. The County Buildings, beyond the hotel, were built in about 1815 by Provost John Ferguson to replace the old tolbooth. On the right, opposite its rival the Tontine, stands the Royal Hotel, built in 1854. It had extensive stables to the east.

7

The row of houses which once stood at the approach to the East Bridge. Only the building at the far left now survives, along with a former smithy which stands behind it. The others, with their little shops on the ground floor, were long ago replaced by a garage. The photograph was taken by D. Gordon, 'Portrait & Landscape Artist and Photographer', probably around 1890.

The St James Market, perhaps the most important of Cupar's eight annual fairs, at the Fluthers. The picture dates from *c*.1910. This fair, like many other medieval fairs in Scotland, died out between the wars. It was held in August, and was for a long time a hiring fair. In 1894 the hiring date for agricultural workers was moved to a fair in October, but the St James Fair remained a ploughman's holiday. The Fluthers was an important public open space belonging to the town. It was protected from development, and used for various purposes including, for many years, the cattle market.

The Old Jail was built in 1814 to replace the insanitary and overcrowded cells in the old tolbooth, where there had been a dark and damp dungeon for criminals and a slightly better cell higher up the tower for debtors. The tolbooth had become so dilapidated that in 1808 two prisoners escaped 'by making a hole in the west wall next [to] the street'. This new jail, however, was never satisfactory, and was replaced in 1843 by another much larger prison further out of the town, at the top of Castlebank Road. The old building was used for a while as the headquarters of the local militia. Then from 1895 to 1988 it was occupied by Watts, the seedsman. 'The Sebastopol Cannon', in front of the prison, was said to have been used at the siege of Sebastopol in 1854, and was displayed in various places around Cupar over the years, including the Moat Hill. In 1872 it was brought out of storage to be erected on the site now occupied by the war memorial. It disappeared during the Second World War, presumably to be melted down for scrap.

Victoria Bridge, Cupar   I am being firmly "held in" here

An example of a range of novelty cards which were once common, where one image and caption was printed over different local views for sale in a variety of towns. Behind the courting couple is the Victoria Bridge. The first bridge on this site was a footbridge provided to serve the Old Jail and built around 1820. A new road bridge was opened by Provost David Watson on 8 June 1901, and was replaced by the present wider bridge in 1993.

Cupar Fair; a large roundabout at the Cross in 1916. Perhaps this fair was held in the Crossgate because the Fluthers was being used by the Lowland Mounted Brigade who were based in and around Cupar at the time. This carefree scene contrasts markedly with the floods of the same year.

The floods of July 1916, looking down North Burnside towards the foot of Lady Wynd. The building on the right was the Burn Square Tanworks, established by James Honeyman in about 1850. There had formerly been a brewery on the site. Honeyman died in 1891, and in 1901 the business was taken over by James Carmichael and Son of Dundee. The works closed in 1951, and the building was later converted into flats.

Peter Ruddiman's shop at 6 Burnside, *c*.1910. Ruddiman was a grocer and spirit dealer and appears in trades directories in 1907 and 1911. After this no more is heard of Peter Ruddiman, but in 1915 there were three separate businesses in the town run by people with this unusual surname, Mrs Elizabeth Ruddiman, presumably his widow, a fruiterer at 118 Bonnygate, his son William, a painter at 61 Bonnygate, and his daughter Miss Maggie Ruddiman, a grocer at 5 West Port.

Alexander Dunlop was a grocer and spirit dealer with a shop at 6 Burnside. This photograph of his delivery van, an Austin K-type registered in Cupar in 1948, was taken outside the shepherd's cottage at Balgove Links, when the van was out on its rounds.

Bonnygate c.1900, with a milk cart in the foreground. The old building on the right on the corner of Ladywynd, end on to the street and with the traditional Scottish crow-stepped gables, was demolished early this century. Beyond it is the tower of the Baptist Church, and, in the distance, Kelly's grocery shop. This building, which stuck out into the street close to the site of the old West Port or gate, was the shop and house of Mrs Kelly, grocer, and was removed when the Co-op was extended in about 1930. Beyond that is St Michael's church, built in 1837 when the congregation outgrew the parish church.

16

The Albert Hotel, Bonnygate, *c.*1900. The hansom cab outside the hotel is being driven by John Thomson, the proprietor, whose name can be seen over the door. An advertisement in 1907 offered 'Commercial Room, Sitting Rooms, and Airy Bedrooms, comfortably furnished, and every endeavour will be used to maintain and even increase the reputation of the House among Travellers'. It also advertised for hire 'Brakes and 'Buses for Pic-Nic Parties'. The photograph was taken by David Gordon.

Donald Ross was born in St Andrews in 1868 and educated at Madras College. At the age of fourteen he was apprenticed to a baker there, and then went to work for a baker in Cupar. In 1892 he set up shop on his own at 42 Bonnygate, and built up a thriving business. He retired in 1925 to enjoy his hobbies of gardening, reading and playing bowls.

Donald Ross's delivery cart, with driver John Brown. Most bakers and butchers in Cupar had carts and made regular deliveries throughout the town and the surrounding countryside. A 1907 advertisement for David Taylor, butcher in Ladywynd, with a photograph of a similar open cart, emphasised 'the complete arrangements of his Van, which is fitted up with all the latest appliances, including a Mincing Machine, whereby the Meat can be minced on the spot, ensuring the same freshness as if bought in the shop'.

Left: John Gilmour's shop at 94 Bonnygate, established in 1907. 'The shop for Picture Post-Cards, Framed Views, Book of Views, Maps and Guide Books, List of Apartments to Let.' As well as a bookseller, Gilmour was a stationer and newsagent, ran a library, and did bookbinding and printing, including printing postcards. Cards of his in this book include the ones on pages 9, 28, 39 and 42. About 1912 he also opened a shop at 24 Bonnygate selling toys and fancy goods.

Right: Drawing of the proposed new YMCA buildings, Ladywynd, Cupar, by C.G. Soutar, Architect, Dundee. Financed in part by a legacy, this building was completed and can still be seen in Lady Wynd, although simpler initials over the door and the date 1906 were substituted for the decorative panel shown here. Unusually for Cupar, the building is of red brick.

This colourful group were photographed collecting funds for the YMCA, 11 July 1916. The Young Men's Christian Association was founded in London in 1844 to promote social and religious work among young men. A hundred years later it had expanded into 56 countries. During the Second World War its work included providing care and education for prisoners of war. The Young Women's Christian Association was founded in 1855.

Looking down Kirkgate and Kirk Wynd from outside the church, *c.*1905. There are no longer any shops in this area. The buildings on the right were later demolished and the area left as open space. Forestairs, such as the one outside the house on the left, provided access to the lighter, dryer living quarters upstairs, while the ground floor of dwellings such as these served as storage or workshop space. Stairs obstructed the road or pavement, and with the growth of motor traffic were gradually removed. In Cupar they lingered longest in the quietest areas, such as here. The spire of the Duncan Institute is visible in the distance.

Looking south down Kirkgate. This undated view by local photographer David Gordon features the chimney sweep with his horse and cart. The first church to stand on this site was built in 1415, the earlier church being to the north-west of the town. The tower is part of the original building, topped with a spire added in 1620. Three bays of the north aisle of the old church survive, and are now used as the session house, but the main part of the church was replaced in 1785 by a plain Georgian structure, designed by a local architect.

The simple shop front of Miss Margaret Williamson, Grocer, 1 Short Lane. Her shop is listed in trades directories between 1900 and 1911. The large stone was to stop carts catching the edge of the building as they turned the corner.

Looking up Kirk Wynd towards the parish church. The corner of the grocery shop featured on the opposite page is to the left, although in this later photograph the grocer is Miss Staig. Many local residents can still remember buying sweeties from Miss Staig's shop.

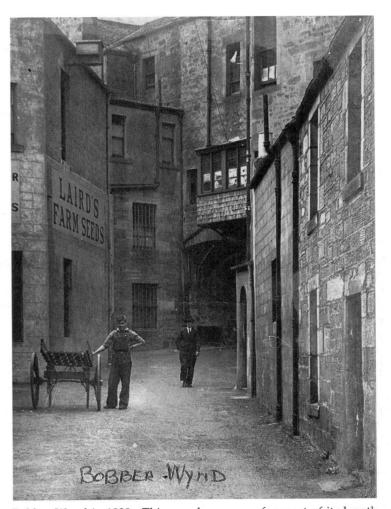

Bobber Wynd in 1939. This wynd now runs for most of its length through a car park. It is shown on the 1642 town plan as a narrow street like Short Lane and Kirk Wynd, lined with buildings right down to the river. The men in the picture are W. Mieckle and D. Rollo.

25

These two views of the Crossgate can be dated to between 1862 and 1870 by the presence of the Corn Exchange and the absence of the Duncan Institute. There is also no Mercat Cross, and there are seats along the street. This photo shows on the left the Waterloo Tavern, and on the right the Blue Bell Inn, later the Station Hotel. Before the building of the Royal and Tontine Hotels during the first half of the nineteenth century, the Blue Bell was probably the smartest hotel in town.

The pictures were taken by Adam Diston, who opened his Talbot Studio in Leven in 1855, and in June 1864 opened a branch studio in Cupar, at 73-75 Bonnygate, opposite the Masonic Lodge. According to a contemporary newspaper 'A.D. begs to state that he has been induced to remove to Cupar by the urgent requests of many friends'.

The interior of the Waterloo Tavern, with its last proprietor, Mr MacDonald. This small pub stood on the corner of Crossgate and Short Lane, on the site of part of the present post office, and can be seen in the Diston photograph on the opposite page.

Crossgate in the early twentieth century. Little has changed except that the handbarrows and carts have been replaced by cars and lorries, and there is no longer a tree in front of Crossgate House. Cupar Savings Bank was founded in 1837, and had premises at 108 Bonnygate. New premises, on the right of this picture, were built in the Crossgate in 1902 at a cost of £1,147. The bank was later taken over by the Trustee Savings Bank. The opposite side of the street is dominated by the unusual spire of the Duncan Institute, opened in 1870. This building was paid for by a legacy from Miss Duncan of Edengrove, for 'the working classes of Cupar, Dairsie and Kilconquhar'. It originally contained two reading rooms, a library, a recreation room, a lecture hall, a billiard room and the museum of the Fifeshire Literary, Scientific and Antiquarian Society.

David Sutherland, merchant, 57 Crossgate. The small boy posed in front of the delivery van is William ('Sus') Sutherland. The photograph was taken in David Sutherland's yard.

Crossgate *c.*1955. The building on the left was occupied by Hood and Robertson between 1887 and 1945, then by Gillies & Henderson, ironmongers, and then by Woolworths, who later built their present shop on the same site.

Geordie Lumsden, hairdresser, at the opening of his shop at 48 Bonnygate in 1932. The man with the briefcase is an insurance agent, and this rather posed photograph was perhaps taken to accompany a write-up of the new shop in the local paper.

Members of the Ayrshire Yeomanry crossing Victoria Bridge. The yeomanry had a camp at Kinloss, just outside Cupar, and in August 1915 held a sports day at Annsmuir, Ladybank, when 'splendid exhibitions of horsemanship were given by the officers and men of the Ayrshires and of the other units of the Lowland Mounted Brigade'. The Lowland Mounted Brigade, which was composed of a number of local yeomanry units, had its headquarters in Cupar during the war, and some of its members can be seen in newspaper photographs of the period on sentry duty outside buildings such as the post office.

BILLY. MASCOT OF 'D' SQUADRON. Q.O.R.G.Y.

DEPARTURE OF 'A' SQUAD. Q.O.R.G.Y.
FOR THE FRONT

Billy, Mascot of 'D' squadron, QORGY, posed for a photograph in 1915 on top of what looks like an upturned tin bath. This and some of the other postcards of this date were produced by Cupar Studios Ltd, South Bridge. Part of the message on the reverse of this card reads: 'My name is next on the list for leave from this troop but there is a rumour just in that leave is practically off owing to so many men being on Brigade duty.'

Departure of 'A' Squadron, Queen's Own Royal Glasgow Yeomanry, from Cupar railway station for the Front, 25 May 1915. These soldiers had a training camp near Cupar and newspaper photographs show their horses grazing on the Carthaugh.

JULIAN AND HER CREW

The tank Julian and her crew, seen here at the Cross in Cupar, toured Scotland selling war bonds. Tanks came into use during the First World War, their development being promoted by Winston Churchill. The first British tanks were used at the Somme on 15 September 1916. By 1918 there were hundreds in use by the British and French, and the first battle between Allied and German tanks took place in April 1918.

Collecting money during Red Cross Week, July 1918, at the junction of Millgate and South Bridge. The Red Cross was established after the Battle of Solferino in 1859, and was formally instituted in 1863 to provide volunteers to tend wounded soldiers. The following year the Geneva Convention laid down rules of behaviour in relation to prisoners of war, and the neutrality of the Red Cross and its role in dealing with battlefield casualties. The role of the organisation soon widened to cover relief of suffering as a result of war, sickness and disaster.

The Adamson Hospital. A legacy from Alexander Adamson in 1866 provided money for the building of a hospital within the parish of Cupar. The trustees were mostly from Ceres, and chose to build the hospital on the edge of the village, albeit just within the parish of Cupar. The hospital opened in 1877, but was always short of money and unpopular because it was so far from the town. In 1901 the building was sold to the Leith Holiday Home, and later became Alwyn House, a training centre for blind people. A new Adamson Hospital was built in Cupar in 1904, with extra funds gathered in memory of local men who died in the Boer War. It has been extended and improved several times since then. According to the Third Statistical Account in 1952 'it can truly be said that there have been few, if any, Cottage Hospitals in Scotland where the patients were better nursed'.

36

Cupar voluntary war workers packing bandages in 1918. The variety of voluntary work undertaken during both the First and Second World Wars was enormous. A related job to this one was the gathering of sphagnum moss, which being spongy and absorbent was used for making dressings.

Cupar Fire Engine. The early years of the French Revolution inspired various political movements in Britain, pressing for greater democracy. One of the more secretive of these organisations was called the United Scotsmen. It was so secretive that little is known about it, but many of its activists were among skilled workers in Fife and Tayside. In December 1797 the United Scotsmen were blamed for two mysterious arson attacks in Cupar. 51 men were arrested and 15 imprisoned for further questioning; 3 of these were sent for trial in Perth. The town of Cupar had been dithering about buying a fire engine for several years, and the arson attacks frightened them into finally making the purchase in 1798. The engine had leather hoses and a pump worked by six men, who were each paid £1 per year and were to test it on the first Saturday of every month. In 1806 the engine was given to the newly established Fife Fire Insurance Company, on condition that they kept it in working order and paid for its use when necessary. The provenance of the engine in this picture is unknown. It is featured on an undated postcard which bears the message: 'Dear Grandma, This is Cupar's new fire engine. What do you think of it? Alistair'.

FISHING ON THE EDEN NEAR CUPAR.

The Eden was described by the minister Thomas Campbell in 1793 as 'a river that never ceases, even in the severest drought, to flow in abundance'. Inhabitants of the town had fishing rights on the Eden, and anyone developing riverside sites had to respect these rights. In the 1870s there were moves to clean up the Eden so that salmon once again swam in it and it could officially be classified as a salmon river, but the plan was given up as it would have been expensive and hard to police. The newspapers in the nineteenth century were full of worries about pollution. There were industrial premises all along the river and its tributaries, and by the 1880s the number of trout in the Eden had been greatly reduced by industrial pollution, domestic sewage, and other effluent such as that from the many pigs still kept in back yards within the town. On the right is one of the many mills which were powered by the water of the Eden. Most of these milled grain, but there were also at various times sawmills, spinning mills, and a snuff mill, which ground tobacco.

Houston's Hillside Foundry. Although a thriving market town, Cupar never became a major industrial centre, although it was home to a number of small industries which either processed agricultural produce or made and repaired agricultural machinery. Most of these were sited either along the Ladyburn, as in the case of the Hillside Foundry, Roger's Mills, and the Burnside Printing Works, or in the area bounded by the Eden, the railway, South Bridge and the Victoria Bridge.

Industries which flourished in Cupar during the nineteenth century included linen factories, a brick and tile works (which moved out to Cupar Muir when the railway was built over its site in 1848), two tanneries, a coach-builders, three breweries, a rope-works, and a number of blacksmiths who gradually in the twentieth century became either agricultural engineers or motor engineers. The Hillside Foundry, later Houston's, was perhaps the largest and best equipped of these. There was also a clay pipe factory at Back Lebanon.

The Barracks, Cupar

'The Barracks' was built in 1842-43 as a prison to replace the Old Jail of 1814 by the Victoria Bridge. The new prison had cells for 33 male and 13 female prisoners, all the necessary facilities such as kitchens, laundry and stores, housing for the governor, matron and warders, and plenty of space for both exercise and work. It ceased to be used as a prison in 1888, and became a barracks for the Territorial Army. During the Second World War it was used by Polish troops stationed in the town.

Polish troops outside the Imperial Bar, St Catherine Street, during World War II. The troops were billeted at various places in and around Cupar, including the Masonic Hall, Castlefield House, the Barracks, Rathcluan, Rumgally and Russell's Mill. Some married local girls and stayed on after the war ended.

Cupar from Old Church Tower

The view from the tower of the parish church in the early twentieth century, showing great uniformity of character among the buildings spread out below. There are none of excessive height or with flat roofs. Carts and a forestair are visible in Kirkgate. The former prison, now the Territorial Army barracks, is visible in the background, standing on a hill to the east of the town. The gardens at the centre of the picture are now a car park. The tower of St John's church, built in 1878, dominates the townscape to the left.

MARTYR'S MONUMENT, OLD CHURCHYARD, CUPAR.

Here lies interred the Heads of LAUR. HAY and ANDREW PITULLOCH, who suffered martyrdom at Edin. July13. 1681 for adhering to the word of GOD & Scotlands covenanted work of Reformation, and also one of the Hands of DAVID HACKSTON of Rathillet who was most cruelly murdered at Edin. July 30th 1680 for the same cause.

1680
Our persecutors filld with rage Their brutish fury to aswage Took heads & hands of martyrs off That they might be the peoples scoff They Hackstons body cutt asunder And set it up a worlds wonder In several places to proclaim These monsters glory'd in their shame
RE-ERECTED
July 15th 1792

This postcard shows both sides of Cupar's most famous gravestone, which stands in the graveyard beside the parish kirk. Laurence Hay, Andrew Pitulloch and David Hackston were three local Covenanters who were executed for their beliefs. Following the Restoration of Charles II, Scotland reverted to an episcopal church (one that is governed by bishops). But there were many who were not happy with this, and support grew for the Covenanters, who advocated a non-hierarchical church structure. In 1679 Archbishop Sharp was murdered at Magus Muir, between Cupar and St Andrews, and there were further acts of rebellion and reprisals at various places throughout Scotland. Hay and Pitulloch, who had signed a paper called a 'Testimony against the evils of the times', were hanged at Edinburgh for their Covenanting beliefs; their heads were sent back to be fixed on the tolbooth of Cupar as a warning to other dissenters. Hackston had been executed the year before and his hand was sent to Cupar for the same reason.

Highland Agricultural Show, Cupar, 1912

Before it settled permanently at Ingliston, the Royal Highland Show was held in locations all over Scotland. From 9-12 July 1912 it was at Kinloss, near Cupar, and many Cupar businesses had stands there. Alexander Honeyman, saddler, whose shop stood at the corner of the Crossgate and the Bonnygate (page 2), did such good business that the following year he took a stand at the Highland Show at Paisley, where he once again made plenty of sales.

Hilton Farm, near Cupar. The arches in the background, known as cart shades, are in a style typical of a late nineteenth century farmsteading. Before the advent of tractors, most farms had several pairs of horses, roughly one pair and one man per 50 acres of arable land. As well as pulling ploughs and other agricultural machinery, horses were harnessed to carts for work around the farm - this one has a load of manure to be taken to the midden or spread on the fields - and for taking goods to and from market.

The *Fife Herald and Journal* shop at 8 Bonnygate, *c.*1905. Robert Tullis (1775-1831), who was born in St Andrews, set up as a bookseller in Cupar in 1797. In 1801 he bought 6-8 Bonnygate, rebuilt it with a shop at the front and a bindery and printing works at the back, and set up home upstairs. He rapidly built up a reputation for accurate and high quality printing, and in about 1808 became printer to the University of St Andrews. In 1809 he guaranteed supplies of good quality paper by buying the paper mill at Auchmuty, near Markinch, a business still trading as Tullis Russell. Thirteen years later he founded the *Cupar Herald*, soon renamed the *Fife Herald*, the first newspaper devoted wholly to Fife. It was printed in a new plant down by the Ladyburn, the Burnside Printing Works. By 1832 the *Fife Herald* had become fairly radical, and the following year the Tory *Fifeshire Journal* was started up in opposition to it. John Innes (1840-1901), worked on both newspapers, and in 1870 founded the *St Andrews Citizen*. He took over the Bonnygate shop and the Burnside Printing Works from the Tullis family in 1879, and in 1892 went into partnership with his brother, trading as J. & G. Innes. Innes acquired the *Fifeshire Journal* and merged it with the *Fife Herald* in 1893. In 1923 the firm took over Westwood's, who had a shop at 20 Crossgate and the Edenside Printing Works.